1 MONTH OF
FREE
READING

at
www.ForgottenBooks.com

By purchasing this book you are eligible for one month membership to ForgottenBooks.com, giving you unlimited access to our entire collection of over 1,000,000 titles via our web site and mobile apps.

To claim your free month visit:

www.forgottenbooks.com/free921254

ISBN 978-0-266-99992-8
PIBN 10921254

VOL. XIII

NO. 9

The Oberlin
Alumni Magazine

JUNE

1917

DIRECTORY AND MISCELLANEOUS

In writing to our advertisers, please mention the Magazine

DIRECTORY AND MISCELLANEOUS

OBERLIN COLLEGE

Legal Title: "The Board of Trustees of Oberlin College"

OBERLIN, OHIO

Henry Churchill King, President

CARNEGIE LIBRARY

DEPARTMENTS

THE COLLEGE OF ARTS AND SCIENCES
THE GRADUATE SCHOOL OF THEOLOGY
THE CONSERVATORY OF MUSIC

The enrolment of students in the College of Arts and Sciences is limited to 1,000 and in the Conservatory of Music to 400; there is no limit in the Graduate School of Theology.

Correspondence with reference to admission to the College of Arts and Sciences and requests for catalogues and books of views should be addressed to the Secretary, George M. Jones; correspondence with reference to admission to the Conservatory of Music should be addressed to the Director, C. W. Morrison; correspondence with reference to the Graduate School of Theology should be addressed to the Junior Dean, G. Walter Fiske.

For the year 1917-18 the College will accept 325 new Freshmen. The Secretary of the College is authorized to issue promises for the reservation of places in the Freshman class. At date of April 20 all of the places for women have been promised, and all but 75 of the places for men.

The Summer Session of 1917 will begin on Friday, June 15; correspondence with reference to the work of the Summer Session should be addressed to S. F. MacLennan, Chairman of the Summer Session Committee.

A PLUM CREEK VIEW

The Oberlin Alumni Magazine

Vol. XIII. Number 9   June, 1917

EDITORS
Helen White Martin, '85; R. H. Stetson, '93

THE OBERLIN ALUMNI MAGAZINE PUBLISHING COMPANY
F. O. Grover, President   George M. Jones, Secretary
R. H. Stetson, Treasurer
Edith Dickson, '74, Business Manager

SUBSCRIPTION PRICE
Oberlin Alumni Magazine, per year . . . $1.00
Single Copies 15
Foreign Subscriptions . . . . 25 cents extra

Communications intended for the editors should be addressed to Mrs. C. B. Martin, 75 Elmwood Place.

Remittances, and material for advertisements should be sent to the manager, Miss Edith Dickson, 172 Elm street. Checks may be made payable to "The Oberlin Alumni Magazine."

Changes in the address of magazines should be sent directly to the Manager of the Magazine. If a change is to be made in the College mailing list notify the Secretary of the College, also.

All material must be received not later than the 15th of each month.

Published monthly except August and September, at the office of the News Printing Company.

Entered as second-class matter at the post office, Oberlin, O., under Act of Congress of March 3, 1879

News and Comment

Thus far the College management has planned to carry out the usual exercises and observances of Commencement. The literary societies have decided to have their reunions as usual, but not to serve a supper. The joint reunion of '96, '97, and '98 has been given up for the year, according to the notice published in this issue. The Commencement Play, " Pomander Walk," will be given, and in general we may expect " Commencement as usual," in spite of war times.

On various occasions President King has urged the students to take thought before plunging into some form of army service. The men ought to see that they make the training and experience which has been given them by society count in such an emergency. And for the underclassmen there is little question that completing their college course is the best possible service they can render at the present time.

The work on the farms has been counted an emergency and any man or woman who could help there has been released on showing definite arrangements for such work. But in general the feeling has been that college men ought not to enlist at present as privates.

The number of men who have left school for various kinds of service is 195. There are a number who have made arrangements and will leave presently; including the ambulance corps of 36. Of these men 35 enlisted in the " mosquito squadron," two went into the cavalry, one into the artillery, eight enlisted in the Cleveland hospital unit, seven in the French Ambulance Service, three in the Navy, one in the English Army, and two in the Officers' Reserve

Corps, and 136 have gone out for farm work.

The colleges have been, of course, centers of interest and excitement in the matter of the war preparations. College people follow events and sense their meaning and students are young, impetuous and foot-loose. The important thing is to direct all the energy and feeling into the right channels.

The War Department has issued a call to the colleges of the country to organize ambulance corps for as early service as possible in France. It may be that these corps will be the first American units which will see service in the war. Oberlin College will be represented by one of these ambulance corps. Some three times the number have signed up for the corps of thirty-six men, for the idea of being a part of an Oberlin corps appeals to the students.

What the effect of the war will be on the attendance at Oberlin is a mere guess at the present time. Much depends on the events of the summer. Probably a number of the upper classmen will fail to return for various reasons. But it is entirely possible that the number of lower classmen will be as large as usual, or even larger. The reaction toward a steadier and a farther vision may have come by fall, and even young people will realize that trained men are essential during the war and after the war, and that no nation and no community can afford to drop all the concerns of civilization to make war, however important waging war may be.

Registration for next year is in progress as we go to press, but cannot give much notion of the attendance in the upper classes for the coming year, as so many of the students are withdrawn, and many of the others are uncertain.

In these days, when so many of the young men of the College are "excused for government service," as the office blanks read, one naturally turns back to other days when colleges all over the country were sending their young men into the Civil War. Of Oberlin College, Professor John Ellis said in August, 1865, "No school in the country, probably, has been so deeply affected by the demands of the war." Permission was given for a meeting of students, in which the citizens also took part, to consider what measures should be taken to respond at once to the President's call for 75,000 men. At a second meeting the roll was opened for enlistment for three months. One hundred and thirty enrolled for a company whose maximum number was 81; $10,000 was pledged by the citizens of Oberlin to assist in furnishing and sustaining those who should go.

This was the "Company C" of the Seventh Regiment, O. V. I. They left within a week for Camp Denison, near Cincinnati, and after six weeks they were in actual service in West Virginia within two months of the time they left Oberlin. They were mustered out just three years later. Of all the things in the remarkable record of the company, perhaps the most striking is the fact that but three of the 150 students in the company at one time and another, died of disease, and two of those deaths were from typhoid fever in a Southern prison. Twenty-eight fell in battle; fifteen, wounded, were discharged; and fifteen were promoted to commissions in other regiments.

During the four years of the war four other companies were formed in Oberlin, containing many students. And of course many of the students enlisted separately. Fairchild, in his History of Oberlin, estimates that about 850 graduates and undergraduates of Oberlin were in the army, of whom about 400 men went out in Oberlin companies.

When one remembers the size of the school and town at that time, it is possible to see how the College responded to the call.

What was the effect on the attendance at Oberlin in the trying times of the Civil War? President Fairchild notes that the enrollment fell off about one-third; but the decrease in the number of men was some two-fifths. During the earlier part of the time it was hard to keep interest in the college work; the North was making every effort to put men in the field and the war news was engrossing. But as the war went on they learned to be steadier. They realized that men of training were essential after the war, and that for the army itself an education was valuable. Remarkable as it seems, in the last two years of a bitterly fought war, the College, which had sent so many men and was so vitally interested in the issues, actually increased its attendance of men as well as of women.

It is evident that after the Civil War a sporadic effort was made to establish military drill at Oberlin. It was voted by the Trustees in August, 1867, to approve the suggestions of the War Department as to military studies and drill. But there is no record of such work being introduced, and apparently the movement died before any actual drill was undertaken.

The financial problem of Dartmouth College is of interest in connection with methods of college finance, which may be considered at Oberlin. A large part of the Dartmouth income hangs on attendance. The Dartmouth Alumni Magazine of May states that the income from tuitions is about $200,000, and from dormitories, in which funds of the college are invested, $37,000. Other invested funds bring in $129,000. This means that Dartmouth is dependent on the students for about two-thirds of the total income, and that ten per cent of the total income is from dormitories. There is danger in a relatively high tuition charge as a source of income. And it is doubtful if Oberlin College can risk building dormitories for the men with endowment funds.

The work of the literary societies for men has been very much crippled by the number of withdrawals. They are continuing their sessions, however, and will hold the "Junior Oratoricals" as usual.

The Northern Oratorical League inaugurated a new system of judges at the league contest of this year.

The instructors in oratory of the several schools graded each orator, with the exception of the representative of his own institution. This system insures the presence of the instructors and makes for common standards; it is possible, however, that in time the type might become somewhat academic.

Northwestern University won first place. The Oberlin man, Mr. W. H. Evans, '18, was given last place. Mr. Caskey characterizes the contest as rather mediocre, and the attendance at this contest, under the auspices of the University of Minnesota, was very small, about 100.

The Union Literary Association is considering the problem of the the support of oratory in Oberlin. The lack of interest and the very small attendance at the Home Contest mean a large annual deficit. With the rise in the cost of printing and the increasing demands of other college interests, the U. L. A. finds it difficult to meet this deficit.

Mr. John L. Severance, '85, has accepted the appointment as honorary marshal at the Commencement Exercises.

Among the noteworthy things at the Commencement of the School of Theology was the address at the Commencement Exercises of Robert E. Speer, Secretary of the Presbyterian Board of Foreign Missions, and the remarkable speech of Dr. Henry M. Tenney at the supper of Commencement evening. An account of the exercises will appear as usual in the Commencement issue of the Magazine.

Nearly one hundred of the two hundred French War Orphans whom the Oberlin community have undertaken to care for have been placed. This means that food is provided for the child by the $36.50 per year raised in America; with a small stipend from the French Government the widowed mother can keep her child instead of having to surrender it to an institution.

The lighting plant operated in Oberlin is inadequate; the contract with the present company expires one year from this September. It is probable that either the College and town will combine in installing a new plant or that the College will maintain its own lighting plant. The load of the new Art Building will be nearly as large as that of all the domestic consumption in the village, and the College is making constantly increasing demands on the lighting service. The re-wiring of Peters Hall and of Severance Laboratory, to be done this summer, will mean more current consumption.

With the increase in the teaching force and material for art study it has come to be possible to offer majors in that department. Some four variations of an art major have been formulated; one is in history of art, one in the practice of art, one in painting and sculpture, and one in architecture.

Calendar

June 1. Final examinations begin.

June 2. Baseball, Ohio State at Oberlin.

June 7. Senior Chapel. Finney Chapel, 4:30 p. m.

June 8. "Pomander Walk," by the Dramatic Association. Finney Chapel, 8 p. m.

June 9. Baseball, Ohio Wesleyan at Oberlin. "Pomander Walk," second performance. Finney Chapel, 8:30 p. m.

June 10. Baccalaureate Sunday.

June 11. Baseball, Varsity vs. Alumni.

The Fatherless Children of France

The appeal in the May number of the ALUMNI MAGAZINE, in behalf of the Fatherless Children of France, has brought some very encouraging responses from the alumni. Up to the morning of May 21st, pledges have been received for the care of fifteen children, and miscellaneous cash contributions amounting to thirty-seven dollars insure a year's support for another, making a total, so far, of sixteen provided for by the readers of the Magazine. In some cases the givers have expressed the intention of continuing their pledges for a second year. Each person pledging a year's support has been sent the name, address, and age of the individual child assigned to him and the occupation of the mother.

The interest manifested has not stopped with the giving. There have been requests for information and material for starting work for the aid of these children in other places. Some of the letters have said that others intended to help and would be heard from soon. All of these expressions show that the cause appeals strongly wherever the urgency of the case is recognized.

One letter asks for an explanation of the statement that the attempt to provide for additional children would stop before next winter, as it would then be too late. The statement was made on the authority of official declarations that it would be useless to extend the work of caring for these children beyond the present season, because those who did not receive help before cold weather would not survive next winter.

It is important that there should be a clear understanding of the difference between the work which has been carried on for the relief of Belgian children and this movement for the aid of the children of France. The announcement has been made that the pledges for the Belgian children are to be cancelled because after the first of June the United States will assume the cost of feeding them. No such arrangement has been made for French children, who must depend upon special contributions.

Pledges and money received from readers of the Magazine are as follows:

For the support of a child one year—Mr. and Mrs. A. T. Hemingway, Kansas City, Missouri; Doctor and Mrs. C. L. King, Pasadena, California; Doctor Robert K. Macklin, Pasadena, California; Doctor Mary E. Hagadorn, Pasadena, California; Lois and Marian Dilworth, Pasadena, California; Mrs. O. S. Kriebel, Pennsburg, Pennsylvania (two children); Miss Emma Gillis, Newtonville, Massachusetts; A Friend; the H. K. Hawley Family, Ames, Iowa; Mrs. Savage, care H. K. Hawley, Ames, Iowa; Miss Laura Alice Biron, Prairie Depot, Ohio; Miss Charlotte Partridge, South Bend, Indiana; Mr. and Mrs. L. MacDaniels, Ithaca, New York; Mrs. Abby Cushman Hine, Mrs. Jean Cushman Bridges, Mr. I. N. Cushman, and Miss Harriet E. Cushman, Chula Vista, California.

Miscellaneous Cash Contributions —Mrs. Nevada D. Hitchcock, Philadelphia; Miss Louie Grove, Ottawa, Illinois; Miss Ruth Hoyman, Rowlesburg, West Virginia; Mr. and Mrs. H. Rogers, Massena, New York; Mrs. F. E. Pratt, Miss H. S. Pratt, Eagle Rock, California; Two Friends.

The total amount of money received in response to the appeal to the readers of the Magazine is $483.63.

The town of Oberlin has responded most liberally to the appeal for the Fatherless Children of France. On the tenth of May $719.50 was forwarded to New York from the Oberlin organization, the receipt of which was acknowledged in the following letter:

Mrs. C. B. Martin, Treasurer,
    Oberlin, Ohio.

Dear Madam:—We beg to acknowledge with heartiest thanks the receipt from you, as Treasurer, of $719.50 for the Fatherless Children of France, Branch of the American Society for Relief of French Orphans.

We have placed the amount to the credit of the organization subject to withdrawal by it or its agents designated to us for such purpose.

Yours very truly,
    J. P. MORGAN & CO.

Names of forty-four children selected from a list of 200 by Oberlin people, who became responsible for their support, were sent at the same time and acknowledged as follows:

Mrs. C. B. Martin,
    Oberlin, Ohio.

My Dear Mrs. Martin:—I acknowledge with appreciation list of 44 children adopted by subscribers to our new Oberlin, Ohio, committee, beginning with the name of Paula Bayle and ending with Leon Ruhlmann. A copy has been sent to Paris.

Sincerely yours,
    M. R. FOWLER,
    Branch Secretary.

Since May 10th, when $719.50 was forwarded to New York from all sources, $651.88 has been contributed and the care of seventy children is now provided for. The first of June will see the number increased.

EDITH DICKSON,
    Chairman Publicity Committee.

The following telegram has just been received in response to a letter asking about the work for the Fatherless Children of France. The report has been circulated that the United States Government is to assume the care of these children. The telegram states clearly the denial of such a report:

New York, N. Y., May 24.
Mrs. C. B. Martin,
Oberlin Ohio:
Government allowance to Belgium Relief Commission and extended scope of work in no way touches our own. This is authoritative. Have written asking Mr. Hoover to make statement in press. Colleges and societies are notifying us funds previously pledged to Belgian children will now come to us. Give statement publicity.

MILDRED FOWLER,
Branch Secretary.

Musical Notes

PIANO RECITAL.
by
MR. OSSIP GABRILOWITSCH.

CHOPIN PROGRAM.

1. Fantaisie—Impromptu
2. Sonata, B minor, Op. 58
3. Six Preludes, Op. 28
   G major, C minor, E flat major
   F major, D flat major, B flat
   minor
4. Nocturne, F major, Op. 15
   Valse, C sharp minor, Op. 64
   Scherzo, B minor, Op. 20
5. Nocturne, E minor, Op. posthumous
   Etude, Op. 25, No. 12

It is doubtful if any pianist of to-day is able to give more genuine pleasure to discriminating listeners than the Russian artist, Gabrilowitsch, who, on May 1st, for a second time in the past two years, delighted an Oberlin audience with a recital from the works of Chopin.

Not so commanding in his personality nor so intense in his emotional make-up as Paderewski; perhaps not so surpassing a technician as Hoffmann, but reminding one of Lhevinne in the exquisite finish of his art, he is able to take his stand with these giants of the present day and feel that he is in his own rightful company.

In his playing one feels a certain something underneath it all—a substratum of broad musicianship, embracing not only an astounding command of the literature of the piano, which enabled him recently in Berlin to present a veritable anthology of the Pianoforte Concerto, performing a cycle of the world's greatest concertos from their beginning to the present day, and showing an amazing catholicity of style, and ability to sympathetically interpret the various times and composers represented; but an unusually broad and comprehensive knowledge of orchestral literature as well, so that he is known in Europe and America as one of the world's really great orchestral conductors. No wonder then that one feels in hearing him that here is no mere pianist, but a musician in all that the word implies.

As an instance of his absolute control over his mental resources, it is interesting to note that the big B minor Sonata that he played, by some considered the most difficult of all Chopin's works, was substituted for the B flat minor Sonata originally on his program at a mere half hour's notice; and too, when he had not played it for months. That he played it so superbly, shows what it is to be really master of one's mind!

While his program was perhaps not so entirely satisfactory as that of last year, which will be remembered for many seasons as a truly remarkable one in all respects, still there were in this one also many great moments.

Nothing could be finer than his playing of the wonderful E major section of the Largo in the Sonata above mentioned—that passage so expressive of half formed wishes and longings, yet with fleeting glimpses of a certain somber happiness, so full of mystery and mysticism that one almost seems to feel the breath of incense as in some darkening cathedral. With what a wealth of beauty of subdued tone and color it was painted before us! And on the other hand, what a delicious bit of objectivity was his reading of the winsome F major Prelude!

Take it all in all, it is very doubtful if there is any one today who gets a deeper hold on the innermost feeling of Chopin as expressed in his works, or whose intellectual grasp of the spirit of Chopin is so true and his rendering so sure.

W. T. Upton.

Communications from Alumni

The University of Rochester,

Rochester, N. Y.

To the Editor of the Alumni
  Magazine:

It has been with considerable interest and some irritation that I have read the discussions that have appeared in the *Review* the past several months. I understand that the student body met recently to express themselves on some of the questions that have from time to time commanded the attention of the alumni. I refer to the tobacco rule, the fraternity question, and the Oberlin system of graduate coaching. In the discussion of these questions, the statement has been made frequently or implied that Oberlin has no red blooded men or that the men of this type are very few; that Oberlin men have not made lasting friendships while in college, and after graduating are unable to make friends; that Oberlin is not looking after the social life of her men to the same degree that other institutions do; and finally, that the action of the Faculty in dropping the fraternity men has alienated a host of its loyal alumni.

I have a feeling that attempts to prove these contentions have been wholly futile and must continue to be so just so long as individuals take sides and give expressions to their opinions without basing their assertions on statistics, thorough investigations or actual experience that would qualify them to speak with authority. These are not questions that anyone interested should feel competent to decide out of his own mind by pure reason without real knowledge of facts and without special study.

To illustrate my point, it has seemed to me that the tobacco question was not a question that should be decided by a man sitting in his office with a pipe between his teeth, or by the man who persistently lights up in street car, subway, or public hall, or even in his own home; nor should it be decided by the individual who is made sick by the aroma of a good cigar or the odor of a stale pipe, nor even by the student who would enjoy his cigaret or pipe, unless these individuals have given thorough study to the question and careful investigation of the facts as to the effects of tobacco.

The tobacco habit, I assume, has long since been taken out of the realm of morals and has become a question of health. But the tobacco question at Oberlin is not a question as to whether it is injurious for a mature man to use tobacco, it is not a question as to whether the use of tobacco hurts a young boy under sixteen. The question of the use of tobacco is a very definite one as I see it: namely, from a health point of view does it injure men from the age of sixteen to twenty-five to use tobacco? This is strictly a scientific question and can best be answered scientifically. It should be answered by the medical profession or by those who have given it scientific study, The opinions of others may be interesting, but have little or no value. The judgments of others may be of aid in deciding other problems which of necessity will arise should smoking be allowed, such as how to provide a smoking room at the gymnasium, because if men must smoke no one would think of depriving them of this pleasure for even an hour during a basket ball game, and they could

not be expected to go outside, where they might be so exposed as to have their physical efficiency lowered. The same problem would have to be met in connection with all recitation and laboratory buildings because red blooded men who smoke must smoke between classes so as to calm their brains, made hot by the rush of red blood. Smoking rooms would have to be provided at the boarding houses because smokers must smoke after meals, or how could they digest their food! They cannot wait until they get outside before lighting their pipes or cigarets.

It seems to me that the same argument applies to the fraternity question. The expressions of those who have not had experience in fraternities in other institutions or have not made a close study of fraternity life in many other colleges may be interesting, but has no weight.

The statement has been made, or the fact implied frequently during the last year, that Oberlin men do not, while in College, make lasting friendships and after graduating they find great difficulty in making friends. Supposedly this lamentable fact is due to the life lived at Oberlin, the social conditions and the lack of a fraternity system. I have been out of Oberlin almost eighteen years and at this writing I can not recall a single Oberlin graduate without many friends. I do not offer this statement as a proof. If this fact is true it ought to be susceptible of statistical proof. Such proof should be furnished by those making the claim. I have no desire to say how this information should be secured. An easy way might be to ask all alumni who have been unsuccessful in making friends to stand, so that we may see who and how many they are.

As compared with other institutions of learning, has the social life of the men been neglected? I would be glad to know in just what way Oberlin has failed so grievously in this matter. Those who are making such a complaint against the conditions at Oberlin should give us the facts. If the social life of the men can be improved and Oberlin can take the lead in this as she has in so many other ways, I am most enthusiastically for it, but the discussion of this point has left me somewhat dazed as I think of it in connection with the many other institutions that I have known.

Are there no red blooded men at Oberlin? Does the life there take the marrow out of their bones? Are the Oberlin men soft and effeminate? I don't believe it, but this is no proof. Those who affirm should give actual facts and statistics. Again I would suggest that those who have been softened arise.

Has the action of the Faculty in the fraternity matter alienated many of the alumni? I don't believe it. I have talked with a great many alumni, some who were at one time in the embryo fraternities, but have yet to find one who is not loyal to Oberlin and some are more loyal than ever. This does not prove the question. Either get the facts or stop offering that statement.

When it comes to the athletic situation, the general argument that I am offering is still applicable.

Physical training is a profession and requires as much study and training as many other professions in a university. The fact that a student has had a course in History, Greek, Art, Latin, or Mathematics, does not necessarily qualify him to give advice that has any particular value as to how to conduct a department, even though he may have graduated. And so I feel that a man who has played on an athletic team is not of necessity qualified to give expert advice as to how to conduct a department of Physical Education, of which athletics is but a part. Here again it would seem that those best qualified to give advice are those who have studied Physical Training from a broad standpoint. I know that many will disagree with my contentions, but I believe they are sound.

Another word about the Oberlin Athletic System and I will subside. I have the greatest respect for the Oberlin system and for the results it has attained. I doubt whether there is another system in the country that can compare with it when its results are studied from all angles. This statement is no proof, but I hope to give some facts that will tend to prove this assertion.

Let me, for the sake of argument, make assertions that probably need no proof. First, everything else being equal, a team drawn from two hundred and fifty to three hundred men should win at least half of its games from teams drawn from institutions of similar size, and possibly a few games from larger institutions.

Secondly, low scholarship standards at an institution should give it an advantage over institutions with higher standards; on the other hand, high scholarship standards would handicap that institution by preventing men from entering, and secondly, by making them ineligible because of failure in scholarship.

Superior coaching should give an advantage and poor coaching should prove a disadvantage. Superior coaching, coupled with low scholarship standards, measured by games won, should be a most excellent combination. Poor coaching and high scholastic requirement, by the same standards, should prove ruinous. Excellent coaching, coupled with high scholastic standards, might be expected to give only moderate success. The assertion has been made and is undoubtedly true that Oberlin has high scholastic requirements. (I rejoice in this fact.) The statement has also been frequently made by some alumni that Oberlin has a poor coaching system. I don't believe it, but I grant it for the sake of argument. Then we have at Oberlin a combination of high scholarship standards, and poor coaching. But what are the facts as measured by the standard of games won? The actual record made by Oberlin is one in which every alumnus should rejoice.

The statistics which have been collected and which I have sent on to the Editor show that in football during the period of 1891 to 1906 Oberlin men won her series from Reserve, Case, Ohio State, Ohio Wesleyan, and Wooster. From 1906-1916 Ohio State was the only team of those mentioned to win the series. From 1886-1916 Oberlin has lost the baseball series to State and Wooster.

In basketball Oberlin has won the series from all these teams. In football, baseball and basketball, Oberlin

has won sixty-two per cent of her games from her biggest rivals.

This indicates a fair amount of success. But consider this fact, too, that the worst athletic seasons Oberlin has ever had in football, were seasons when the teams were coached by a Yale, a Pennsylvania and a Columbia man. It may be a coincidence that no team coached by an Oberlin man has even approached the record of failure made by the teams coached by these men brought in from the outside. A Harvard man left Oberlin after some success and became a failure as a coach. Was his success at Oberlin due to his coaching or to the playing of such men as Gray, MacDaniels and others?

Now if we take away from our statistics the results of the lean years when Oberlin was coached by foreign men, we will find that the record made by the graduate coaches stands forth in a still better light. Basketball, the sport in which Oberlin has made her best record, has been entirely handled by Oberlin men.

According to the 1916 catalogues. I find that all the institutions with which I have compared the Oberlin record have a larger enrollment of men than Oberlin, with the exception of Kenyon.

For the sake of argument, I have assumed that Oberlin has had a poor coaching system, a high scholastic standard, and she has actually fewer men, and yet in spite of all this the facts show that she has met with real success in athletics, even when we judge this success by the crude standard of games won.

Explain it however you will, I explain it on the ground that the Oberlin athletic system has been most efficient.

The question of securing a coach for a long term is an interesting one. If the right sort of a man can be secured and he is willing to take the risk of losing his position while in his prime because of howls from the alumni when conditions for a few years prevent his turning out a successful team, I hope that he will be appointed, but not because the present system has been a failure.

Personally, I have such faith in the Director of Athletics that I am content to accept his judgment on any athletic policy that he may decide upon, as I do the policy decided upon by the heads of other departments. Inasmuch as money speaks louder than words, I would suggest a little more of that, so that the athletic plans which have been so long contemplated can be put into actual operation.

Perhaps no injury has been done to Oberlin so far by the discussions, but it is only a question of time before harm will come. I for one am for getting behind and boosting

EDWIN FAUVER.

Athletics

Since the football season Oberlin has slowly but surely been regaining her accustomed place in athletics. Not a game was won in football. In basketball the team was more successful, winning three games and losing games to Denison, Reserve and Buffalo, only by close margins. The spring season has been correspondingly more successful.

The baseball team lost the first game to Reserve, 9-2, and won the second from Baldwin-Wallace, 13-8. Meanwhile the track team was far from idle, inasmuch as it upset the "dope" completely in the triangular meet with Case and Wooster. The results of that meet were, Oberlin 71½ points. Case 49, Wooster, the expected champion, 41½ points. Oberlin's winners in the events were: Martin in the 100-yard, time, ten flat; Captain Fall in the mile and two-mile in comparatively slow time; Farquhar in the 220 in 22⅖ seconds; P. B. Sheldon in the half-mile, time 2:09⅕; Bailey in the broad jump with a dis-

tance of twenty feet nine inches; D. M. Sheldon in the javelin, with a distance of 128 feet 10½ inches.

The results of the various teams on Saturday, May 12, are best told by the *Plain Dealer* of May 15, under the heading, " Oberlin Comes Back," and which in substance follows: " Oberlin has come back. Almost in a single day the crimson and gold athletes have placed themselves in line for honors in the annual spring conference races, when the track, tennis and baseball squads achieved three distinct surprises and made the most significant records of the year. While the track team was giving Ohio State one of the biggest surprises in the annual dual meet between the schools Saturday, the baseball team sent Case home badly beaten, and the tennis team registered a shut-out over Kenyon's championship pair of 1916. The Ohio State dual meet resulted in a 61-56 defeat, but it was virtually a triumph for the inexperienced Oberlin team. With a single exception it was the hardest race an Oberlin team has ever given State in the dual games and it makes the chances for an Oberlin victory at the Big Six games two weeks later seem the best since Oberlin last won the annual classic in 1910." The Chapel bell has been playing the sweetest music lately.

The feature of the track meet was the work of Captain Deke Fall, who, after winning the mile in 4:23, breaking the Big Six record, won the two-mile, and then as last man in the relay, won that event by running his quarter in 51⅖ and beating State's best by fifteen yards. Martin again won the hundred in ten flat. Doty won the 220 in 2:31; Bailey won the broad jump with 20 feet 11 inches; Jones took the high jump with 5 feet 7; in addition Laity managed to get over 11 feet 4 inches in the pole vault.

The tennis team which defeated Kenyon consisted of Wilder and Marvin. Marvin defeated Schaefer, Kenyon's star, who has been a Big Six finalist for three years. The members of the Physical Training department, who have charge of the spring athletics, are L. F. Keller, baseball; H. C. Curtis, track; D. P. Maclure, tennis.

D. P. MACLURE.

Medical Training for Women

548 Engineers' Building,
Cleveland, Ohio,
May 11, 1917.

To the President of the Oberlin
College Alumnae Association.

My Dear Madam:—We take the liberty of informing you that Dr. Charles Thwing, President of Western Reserve University, has given us unofficial notice that if ten women, possessing a college degree, should make application to enter, the law or medical schools which do not now admit women would probably open their doors to us in the fall. The securing of ten girls is the serious prerequisite.

We are bringing this matter to your attention in the hope that some of your alumnae, if they knew that these schools might be open to them, would decide to follow one or other of these professions.

May we ask you kindly to present this matter to all of your alumnae by the earliest possible means, and to ask any girls who wish to make application for entrance to notify us at the address above?

In view of the world war, and the departure of our surgeons to France, it may be that the women doctors will have to carry on the greater part of the nation's health work for the next few years. We therefore feel that the community will be rendered a great service if the Medical School of Western Reserve University, one of the finest in the country, should be opened to women and if more women were to study medicine.

We therefore trust that we may ask your coöperation in securing this opportunity for women.

Very sincerely yours,

The Committee of the Alumnae of the Association of the College for Women upon Securing the Opening of the Law and Medical Schools of W. R. U. to Women.

Announcement of Fellowship Appointments

The Committee on Graduate Study has announced the names of the successful candidates for the three Fellowships. They are as follows: The Johnston Fellowship, the gift of the L. L. S. Alumnae Association, was awarded to Miss A. B. Doerschuk, 1906, Miss Elisabeth Martin, alternate. Miss Doerschuk has been a member of the Faculty of Oberlin College and Assistant Dean of College Women since 1911. She is now at Columbia University. She has been granted a leave of absence for two years.

The Aelioian Fellowship, the gift of the Aelioian Alumnae Association, was awarded to Miss Theresa J. Sherrer, 1914, A.M. 1915. Miss Sherrer is a member of the Faculty at Martin College, Pulaski, Tennessee. Miss Edith S. Gray, 1911, A.M. 1912, a student in the graduate department at the University of Chicago, is alternate. The Gilchrist-Potter Prize Fund was awarded to Miss Rossleene M. Arnold, 1916, a graduate student in the department of chemistry at Oberlin. Miss Elisabeth Martin, 1916, is the alternate appointment.

Philadelphia College Club

Women graduates of Oberlin College and those who have successfully completed one year of the regular academic course are eligible for membership in the College Club, 1300 and 1302 Spruce Street, Philadelphia, Pennsylvania.

The annual dues are $10 for resident, $5 for non-resident members.

The entrance fee of $10 is remitted to those who apply within one year of graduation.

Any one who would like to apply for membership or who wishes information about the Club is asked to write to Miss Doris Fenton, 1319 Spruce Street, Philadelphia, Pennsylvania.

L. L. S. of New York

The New York Branch of L. L. S. held a luncheon at the Cosmopolitan Club, 133 East 40th Street, New York City, on May 5, 1917. The guest of honor was the well known writer and lecturer, Mrs. Kate Upson Clark, who gave a witty account of her one meeting with President Finney. The other speakers were Mrs. J. F. Johnson, Miss A. Beatrice Doerschuk,

Miss Genevieve N. Carr and Miss Leora G. Field. A telegram of greeting was read from Miss Katharine Wright, the president of the General Association, and a report from Mrs. G. A. Lawrence, the treasurer. Mrs. John R. Rogers, the president of the New York Branch, presided, and there were twenty members present.

Important Notice for Women's Societies

The women's five literary societies have made a change in their programs since the announcements in the Commencement bulletin. In view of the war, the usual banquets held by each society will not be given, but the proposition will be made to all that the money usually spent in this way be given to the War Relief Work among the children of France, that the Love Feasts be this year in deed as well as in name.

The alumnae and members of the various societies will meet at 6:45 as follows: Aelioian at Mrs. E. I. Bosworth's, 78 South Professor Street; Phi Alpha Phi, at Baldwin Cottage; Sigma Gamma at Keep Cottage; Tau Kappa Epsilon, at the Women's Gymnasium; and L. L. S., at Talcott Hall. At 8 o'clock all are asked to assemble at the Women's Gymnasium, where a unique program of interest will be given.

Postponement of Joint Reunion

The joint reunion of the classes of '95, '96, '97 and '98 has been postponed till after the close of the war. This action was taken by the joint committee after a postal card vote of all the classes had been taken. '95 and '98 will hold no reunion this year except the usual gathering of the members who attend Commencement.

'96 will have its headquarters at Mrs. L. C. Klinefelter's, 137 Elm Street, and a good representation of the class will return.

So many of the members of '97 have planned to come back that it has been decided to hold their regular twentieth reunion this year. All unnecessary expense will, however, be avoided and plans are being made for a reunion on a much simpler scale than that contemplated before the declaration of war. The class headquarters will be at the Goodrich House, where reservations are already being made.

Alumni News

PHI BETA KAPPA ELECTIONS.

The following members of the senior class were elected to membership in Phi Beta Kappa:

Harold D. Allen, Wilton, Connecticut; Dorothy E. Birkmayr, Toledo, Ohio; Eda H. Bredehoft, Danbury, Ohio; Katherine B. Bushnell, Mansfield, Ohio; Nina R. Clay, Oberlin, Ohio; Laura Dasef, Barberton, Ohio; Uarda Evans, Cassville, N. Y.; Richard R. Fauver, Lorain, Ohio; Florence Hiatt, Peoria, Illinois; Elizabeth J. Hill, Milford, Ohio; Donna L. Mallory, Toledo, Ohio; Frances B. Nobis, Amelia, Ohio; Harlan R. Parker, Cleveland, Ohio; Beatrice E. Paton, Chardon, Ohio; John W. Pence, Hamilton, Illinois; Amy L. Pendleton, Corbin, Virginia; Esther D. Porter, East Jordan, Michigan; Marion M. Root, Oberlin, Ohio; Willis H. Scott, Chicago, Illinois; Elbert M. Shelton, Wakeman, Ohio; Mary T. Sherwood, Oberlin, Ohio; Walter B. Smith, Ashley, Ohio; John E. Stone, Salem, Ohio; Mary F. Tenney, Ada, Ohio; Margaret M. Wilson, New York, New York.

Class of 1911—Ralph E. Rindfusz, Urbana, Illinois.

Class of 1916—Esther F. Schultz, Bellevue, Pennsylvania.

OBERLIN MUSICAL CLUB OF NEW YORK CITY.

The Oberlin Musical Club, which meets each month with Maude Tucker Doolittle, 606 West 116th Street, New York City, is closing a successful and interesting year. In April Helen Morrison assisted and received a rousing reception. She recited some Noyes poems and a scene from the "Romancers" by Rostand. Her own charming personality and her natural conception of her art, so entirely free from affectation, have made her a favorite always. Miss Paine of Minneapolis was the musical artist, playing piano solos by Bach, Chopin and Debussy. Miss Paine was a former classmate of Mrs. Doolittle's in Berlin and the Club were happy to welcome her.

In May Mrs. Catherine Burtt Carter and Mary Blue, a teacher and pupil at Damrosch Institute of Music, New York, rendered a delightfully artistic musical program at the close of which Mr. Henry Gaines Hawn, president of the School of Speech Arts, Carnegie Hall, gave an interesting talk and a few dramatic recitations.

The last meeting in June will be given by Isabelle Dennison, Blossom Wilcox and Margaret Jamieson, the latter having given a successful recital in Aeolian Hall, New York, during the past winter. The active club members are all doing public musical work of various kinds in New York and reflecting honor on their alma mater.

OBERLIN ALUMNI ASSOCIATION OF ILLINOIS.

Oberlin alumni and former students to the number of 140 met at the Hotel La Salle, Chicago, on March 31, for the annual luncheon of the Oberlin Alumni Association of Illinois. This gathering, while not quite so large as some which have been held in Chicago, brought together an unusually large number of recent graduates and students, and included quite a few living some distance out of Chicago. Mr. W. F. Bohn of Oberlin was the guest of honor.

The program was a very informal one. The topic, "Live Issues at Oberlin Today," furnished the basis for three frank, thoughtful and altogether enjoyable talks by recent graduates—John W. Herring, 1914; Grover C. Clark, 1914; and Donald M. Love, 1916. Their remarks touched largely, of course, upon the social life of the men in Oberlin at present, and while some friendly criticism was made and a few changes suggested, the attitude of all the speakers, as well as of those who listened, judging by their approval of the talks, was one of full and cordial support of the administration and the ideals which it is striving to maintain.

Mr. Bohn brought us not only welcome greetings from Oberlin, but gave us as well a full conception of present activities there; the wise and careful study constantly being applied to student life to render it more efficient and helpful;

the doings of numerous Oberlin men and women throughout the country and the respect and esteem which is accorded everywhere to Oberlin and its graduates. Owing to the fact that the president of the association, Dr. R. A. Millikan, of Chicago University, had been called to Washington for service with the government, Mr. Fredrick C. Chamberlain, the vice-president, presided.

Following the speaking there was a brief business session and the following officers were elected for the ensuing year:

President, Dr. R. A. Millikan; vice-president, Frederick C. Chamberlain; secretary-treasurer, Ruth G. Nichols; executive committee, Mrs. F. E. Smith, chairman, Mercy B. Hooker, Arthur Baker, R. T. Miller, Jr.

The program closed with the spirited singing of Oberlin songs and "America," Lawrence Schauffler presiding at the piano.   RUTH G. NICHOLS,
Secretary.

ALUMNI OF WESTERN PENNSYLVANIA.

The Oberlin Alumni Association of Western Pennsylvania held their annual meeting May 2 at the Fort Pitt Hotel in Pittsburgh. The meeting took the form of an informal supper, with President King as the honor guest and only speaker. The officers for the past year were all re-elected for the coming year: Arnaud Marts, 1910, president; Karl Zoeller, 1899, vice-president; Helen Hudson, 1915, secretary and treasurer.

This association has met several times during the winter, at luncheons and other informal gatherings. In February the women of the association entertained the men at the College Club rooms, presenting a one-act play, "The Burglar." Those taking part were Zoe Marts, Irene Raber, Grace Farrell, Erma Jones and Helen Hudson. A few weeks later the younger members of the association enjoyed a chicken supper and informal dance at "The Pines."

NEW YORK ALUMNI MEETING.

The annual meeting of the Oberlin College Alumni Association of New York took place at the Whitehall Club Saturday evening, April 28. A spirit of serious and business-like attention to the main purpose of the evening was evident from the moment one entered and began conversation with one group after another of old friends as they stood about the rooms exchanging greetings and talking over the change that had been made in the program. This was made only about one week before the occasion, and when the revised · invitation proposed cutting the cost of the tickets from two-fifty to a dollar and giving to military equipment for the undergraduates rather than spending for a dinner and decorations the spirit of Oberlin was aroused and one's blood flowed faster as he felt that here had been grasped one opportunity for service.

About nine o'clock all joined in singing the " Star-Spangled Banner," after which President C. C. Johnson, '99, introduced Miss Caroline Lowe's ('91) male quartette, which ably rendered a number of selections. Miss Helen Morrison, '12, then recited an Anti-Suffrage Monologue, to the great amusement of the audience, and as an encore, " Inquiring about Trains." Miss Blossom Wilcox, '13, sang "Like a Rosebud" by LaForge, "Fantoche" by DeBussy, and "The Open Secret" by Woodman. The third was especially enjoyed, and an encore, "An Irish Folk-Song," most of all.

Then came the loyal and stalwart pillar of Oberlin College and Oberlin Graduate School of Theology, Professor William J. Hutchins. His name had been on the invitation and all were eager to hear him. And there was no disappointment. He never fails to bring and to drive home a spirit of just pride for Oberlin. Already the best endowed college in the United States, gifts are still flowing in, and only a few days since an Akron man, in giving ten thousand dollars, told Mr. W. F. Bohn, Assistant to the President, that he wanted to help students who were working their way because he liked to see the way they were doing it at Oberlin.

Professor Hutchins recalled some of the advantages of freedom from fraternities of which other colleges are trying to rid themselves. He spoke of the wholesome effect of co-education despite some dispersed attention. He said that upon comparison of the statistics of thirty-one colleges in that part of the United States, Oberlin was found to be the most successful in holding students throughout the college course. He reminded us of her wonderful producing power for various great causes. Eight hundred men were contributed to the Civil War. One-sixth of the staff of the American Board of Foreign Missions is composed of Oberlin men and women. Recently $3,700 was given by the College to the Shansi Mission and $3,500 to the War Relief Fund.

Lastly he referred to remarks of Herman Hagedorn, who may be called the Poet Laureate of the Phi Beta Kappa Society—how he had called Oberlin the college with a glow on it, and had said that in passing from one institution to another many colleges seemed mere machines, but Oberlin had a soul.

The main address of the evening was given by Mr. Paul D. Cravath, '82. President Johnson introduced him as an institution. To those who were not present it is impossible to convey on a printed page the impression received by those who heard him! Just returned from between the lines on the Somme, having had close association with the leading men of England and France, ready and eminently capable of imparting impressions and information he had received, any alumnus in New York who did not take the pains to hear him has lost an opportunity.

It was only by a chance that he went to the front, because for some time past all persons not directly connected with the army have been forbidden. One evening he was at table as one of a group of a dozen men, among whom were Lloyd George, Bonar Law, Winston Churchill and some of the leading military officers. Such ignorance of the real situation was displayed that one of the generals told Mr. Cravath that in order to correct the wrong impressions he was getting there he should go to the front.

The next morning Mr. Cravath called on the general, asked him if he really meant what he said, and as a result received a "white pass."

They crossed the Channel on a transport with a thousand men and were convoyed by two torpedo-boat destroyers. They traveled through congested France to G. H. Q. (general headquarters), a sweet little village about fifty miles back from the trenches. Men there were in uniform, but here was no sound of cannon and the place was quiet enough to have been at peace. Here as in England each afternoon they take their tea.

Near the front tents are avoided as much as possible and in every village soldiers are quartered in the public buildings, houses and barns. They are everywhere. For miles back from the trenches fields, hills and valleys swarm with men. From a distance it appears like a gigantic ant-hill, but on closer approach all the movements are seen to be coördinated. War is a business. The Standard Oil Companies with seventy-five thousand, or the United States Steel Corporation with two hundred thousand men are pigmy concerns beside this body of men. But they are no better organized. A gigantic and horrible business. The object is to kill, destroy, humiliate.

For miles back of the heavy artillery Mr. Cravath thought there was not a square rod of ground which had not been torn by some missile. Villages had become mortar and dust and the open fields were raised in ridges. The whole country was plowed. Some holes would be fifty or a hundred feet in diameter, and one had a canvas stretched over it and was used as a hospital. From one spot where he was, both the Central and Entente forces were firing at each other over his head.

Back at G. H. Q. all was quiet, and at lunch with General Haig there was not an interruption during the whole hour, although a sanguinary battle was in progress. He showed Mr. Cravath maps and plans giving the positions and detailed information of the movements of both sides.

Later Mr. Cravath was permitted to stay in a room where some ten men conducted a battle. There was no talking.

Messages came in, several a minute. The officers made notes on their charts and sent out return messages and orders. They worked with intensity until evening, when the battle was over, and the generals went about the village as any business man would after his day's work. That day three thousand men were consumed in order to inflict a similar loss upon the enemy and capture less than a square mile.

This great business of destruction is conducted with the same quiet calm as any great industrial corporation. The spirit of war prevails to such an extent that even where shells are bursting all sense of fear is absent. In the hospitals Mr. Cravath heard never a groan or whimper, although he saw thousands of wounded. Three or four thousand a day are sent back to England. Care of the sick is thoroughly organized. Nine surgeons operated on thirteen hundred men in one day.

The question arises, Is the square mile captured per five thousand men lost worth the cost? This has been about the rate during recent victories. Mr. Cravath believes it pays. Wisely or not, terms announced by the Allies are the complete humiliation of Germany. The only way to accomplish this, he believes, is insistently and unremittingly to pound, pound, pound, until they are subdued and broken down. When, and perhaps whether, this will occur, depends largely upon the psychology of the German people. Mr. Cravath believes the war will last at least two or three years. It may take not only seven billions of our money, but seventy billions, and hundreds of thousands of our men. Russia is disorganized and there is possibility that Germany will soon have Petrograd or Odessa. This would make her useless to the Allies, but would not necessarily end the war. The English and French will, he believes, keep pounding till the German morale is gone.

Our only safe course, he says, is to assume that the Allies will need not only our ships, munitions and money, but our men. There is going to be a shortage of food. With modern civilization it is almost impossible to imagine a food famine, but such faces us when we have two million men under arms.

Mr. Cravath spoke of the toughness of the moral fiber of the English and of the fact that though her first call was for but one hundred thousand men, and at the end of the first year people had no thought of raising more than five hundred thousand, yet she now has an army which compares with that of France. More lives have already been lost, he says, than in all other wars of civilized nations during the past century.

In closing, Mr. Cravath expressed the hope that the men now drilling at Oberlin might go to the front, and with a victorious army of the Allies, triumphantly cross the Rhine.

Plans were made for raising a fund to assist in the military training at Oberlin.

The following officers were elected for the ensuing year:

E. A. Lightner, '03, president; Orville C. Sanborn, '02, vice-president; Mrs. Augustus Healy, '92, vice-president; J. H. Wilson, '12, treasurer; T. Nelson Metcalf, '12, recording secretary; Herman Nichols, '14, corresponding secretary.

Alumni Personals

1867.

Twinsburg, in Summit County, Ohio, has sent many students to Oberlin and has several in college now. Rev. R. T. Cross has been pastor of the Congregational Church there for several years. He retires now from the active pastorate, but will continue to live at Twinsburg. During the past three years he has prepared genealogical sketches, a thousand or more, of all the families that have lived in Twinsburg since its settlement in 1817. These sketches form the larger part of the Twinsburg Centennial History that has just been published, a large illustrated book of about 560 pages. No other township in Ohio has prepared and published such a list. Centennial exercises will be held August 5-11, a pageant being the chief feature.

1870.

Dr. James F. Baldwin of Columbus, Ohio, was elected president of the State Medical Association, which held its annual meeting the middle of May at Springfield.

1875.

The *Illinois Law Review* for May, 1917, contains a short article by Merritt Starr of Chicago, entitled "Individualist and Social Conception of the Public." It is a review of the annual address of President Elihu Root to the American Bar Association, delivered in Chicago August 30, 1916. Mr. and Mrs. Starr's son, Philip C. Starr, lately commissioned as Lieutenant in the Canadian Overseas Expedition, is about to sail for the front.

Thomas McClelland, who has been president of Knox College, Galesburg, Illinois, since 1900, has just tendered his resignation to that institution, the same to take effect at the close of the college year. In commenting on President McClelland's resignation, *The Knox Student* says:

"The administration of President McClelland covers a period of seventeen years, perhaps the most significant period in the history of the college. It is not too much to say that it has seen the development of the new Knox. The statement made by a member of the Board of Trustees at the recent Founders' Day banquet, that henceforth President McClelland must be recognized as one of the founders, was eminently appropriate. The material increase in the equipment and endowment, amounting in round numbers to a million dollars, secured through the wise planning and unremitting effort of President McClelland, is a fact which speaks for itself. It is plain to those who are familiar with the situation of the college financially at the beginning of this administration, that its very existence was in peril because of its lack of resources.

"But the recognition of Dr. McClelland's service to Knox College should by no means be limited to the financial side of his work. Parallel with the visible enlargement in material equipment, both in buildings and endowment, there has

been also a notable development in the position of the college as a conspicuous factor in the educational work of the middle west.

"Indeed, the success of the financial campaign was made possible by the academic standing of the college, which brought the endorsement of such agencies as the Carnegie Foundation for the Advancement of Teaching, and the General Education Board; and this recognition is due in no small measure to the educational policy of the President."

1883.

Rev. Charles D. Brower has been called from Glen Forest, Illinois, to the church at Geneva, Illinois.

1884.

Miss F. I. Wolcott attended the meetings of the American Association of Collegiate Registrars, held April 25 to 27, at the University of Kentucky, Lexington. More than sixty colleges and universities were represented.

1889 O. T. S.

Rev. Herbert O. Allen is pastor of the Congregational Church at Osage, Iowa.

Rev. and Mrs. William L. Curtis of the Japan Mission of the American Board, are at home on furlough. Address, care A. B. C. F. M., 14 Beacon Street, Boston, Massachusetts.

Rev. William A. Griffiths has resigned his charge in Cleveland, Ohio, and has accepted the call to the Congregational Church at Bristol, Wisconsin.

1890.

Professor C. A. Kofoid, until recently a member of the Faculty of California University, is now on the Committee on Zoölogy of the National Defense Council of the National Academy of Science.

1891.

Dr. Robert G. Millikan of Chicago University has been appointed vice-chairman of the government's National Research Council, with headquarters at Washington.

1892.

Charles C. Kirkpatrick is now at 17-18 Flatiron Building, New York City, where he represents the Town Development Company.

1893.

Rev. and Mrs. Theodore T. Holway will spend the coming five months in the mountains near Asheville, North Carolina, where Mr. Holway will serve as pastor of one of the churches until the newly elected pastor arrives.

1893 O. C. M.

Professor Arthur E. Heacox has completed a new book entitled "Harmony Training at the Keyboard," which will be published in the early fall by the Arthur P. Schmidt Company of Boston. It will appear in two volumes as a part of Schmidt's Educational Series.

1900 O. T. S.

Rev. Frank G. Beardsley has been called from Keokuk, Iowa, to be pastor of the First Church, Aurora, Illinois.

1901 O. T. S.

Rev. and Mrs. Charles Elliot moved from Wyanet, Illinois, to Davenport, Iowa, in November, 1916. Berea Church is the largest Congregational Church in Davenport.

1902.

Mr. A. W. Monosmith, who for a number of years has been in the timber business in Oregon, is now "land man" with the Cloverland Timber Company of St. Paul, Minnesota, which has holdings of over one hundred thousand acres of land in Northern Michigan. He is residing at 129 Hollywood, Oberlin, Ohio.

1904.

Richard T. F. Harding, who been night editor of the *Cleveland Plain Dealer*, is with the officers' reserve training camp at Fort Benjamin Harrison, where he will take the three-months' course of drill and instruction, after which he will take the examination for a commission in the reserve corps.

1905-1906.

Walter Husted Wolfe, the two-year-old son of Mr. Jesse B. Wolfe and Mrs. Clara Husted Wolfe of Shansi, China, died April 6, 1917, of pneumonia after a short illness.

1906.

H. H. Doering has been recently appointed sales manager by the Baker R. and L. Company for the Rauch and Lang electric motor cars.

Franklin P. Schaffer was again chosen Grand Prelate of the Grand Commandery of Knights Templar of the State of Oklahoma at the Annual Convocation held at Tulsa, Oklahoma, on April 20, 1917.

Miss Faith Parmelee is under appointment of the Foreign Department of the National Board of the Y. W. C. A. for Association Work in India. She sails August 21 on the S. S. "Korea Morn" from San Francico, will spend three weeks in Japan en route and reach Bombay the latter part of October. Her address there will be care Y. W. C. A., 170 Hornby Road, Bombay, India. There are now twelve American secretaries in the Y. W. C. A. in India.

1908.

Mr. and Mrs. Ray L. Edwards announce the birth of Jean Alice Edwards, April 29, 1917.

1910.

George Wainwright Hatanaka and Miss Kimino Watanabe were married at Okayama, Japan, December 12, 1916. Mr. Hatanaka is now pastor of the largest of the six Congregational churches in Kyoto, Japan.

1910-1911.

Born, to Dr. Whitelaw R. Morrison and Helen Barber Morrison, a daughter, Ruth, on March 19, 1917, in Shanghai, China. Dr. and Mrs. Morrison and family are returning to America in July, Dr. Morrison having completed his contract with the Government Institute of Technology.

1910-1915.

Mrs. Warner P. Sutton of Madison, Ohio, announces the marriage of her daughter, Enid Bancroft Sutton, and Mr. Wilbur Fridolf Swan, on Saturday, May 19, 1917, at Madison, Ohio. Mr. and Mrs. Swan will make their home in Sioux City, Iowa.

1910-1916.

Mr. and Mrs. William S. Ament will spend the summer at Frankfort, Michigan, where Mr. Ament will be director of athletics and Mrs. Ament will be the pianist for the season of 1917 of the Congregational Assembly.

1911.

Born, to Mr. and Mrs. Solon H. Barnard (Mabel De Golyer Barnard), March 25, 1917, a son, Howard Fitch.

Mr. R. A. Keller and Mrs. Bess Morris Keller announce the birth of a son, John Morris, January 27, 1917, at Peoria, Illinois.

1912.

Miss Elma Pratt will continue as proprietor of Dorset Inn, Dorset, Vermont, during the summer season of 1917. Miss Alice Barber will hold the position of secretary to Miss Pratt. Dorset Inn will be open from June 15th, through October.

Miss Esther C. Andrews has accepted a position at the Red Cross headquarters, Metropolitan Building, New York City. Her home address is Barbour House, 330 West 36th Street.

Ernest R. Smith is on his way to Central and South America to do field geology for a large corporation. His address is care Sinclair, Central American Oil Corporation, Port Limon, Costa Rica.

R. C. Booth has accepted a new position with the A. B. Kirschbaum Company of Philadelphia, where he will have charge of the Employment and Welfare Work.

Harry B. Yocom, who expects to complete the work for his Ph.D., in Zoölogy in the University of California at the end of the summer session, has been appointed Professor of Zoölogy in Washburn College, Topeka, Kansas.

Rev. Robert G. Armstrong is pastor of the Congregational Church at Spencer, Massachusetts.

CHARLES R. HOWLAND.

The *Rock* is a twelve-page monthly published at the Pacific Branch United States Disciplinary Barracks, Alcatraz, of which Major Charles Howland is Commandant. The May number contains a summary of the work done in the School of Instruction in this institution of correction. Of the 450 men in confinement for terms usually of a year to three years, 372 are taking grade school work. Seventy-four are taking extension courses in work of about high school level; shop arithmetic and Spanish are the favorite subjects.

There are courses in vocational training, and 381 men are enrolled for training in a wide variety of trades, including the ordinary ones, and one or two which smack of military life like " Barracks Mess," " Band," and " Ordnance Repair." Some 419 men have taken such training to date. Twenty-eight completed the course during the month and employment was secured at release for seven. About one-fourth of the men so trained have been secured employment.

This month's installment of the report of the Commandant gives some idea of the study of the cases and the effort to do what can be done practically and scientifically for them. It is interesting to note that the ordinary form of the Binet Simon tests have not proved at all satisfactory with these adults, as proved by their records in school work. The surgeon cites the unusual ignorance of many of the men as an explanation of failure to pass the adult tests. But recent investigations have shown that they are unsatisfactory with many adults in ordinary life. The psychiatric history of each case is secured. It is evident that an intelligent effort is made to diagnose each case.

1913.

Born, to Mrs. Margaret Jordan Topliff and Mr. Harrison F. Topliff, a daughter, Margaret Ellen, May 4, 1917, at Willimantic, Connecticut.

1914.

Miss Alice Coffin, who the past year has been teaching at Amherst, Ohio, has resigned and accepted a position at Xenia, Ohio.

Rev. Lawrence B. Robertson has been called to Pilgrim Church, Madison, Wisconsin.

Harold M. Metcalf was admitted to the Bar in May.

John W. Love gave a talk to the Press Club the evening of May 3, on "The Trials and Triumphs of a Correspondent." Mr. Love is assistant state editor of the *Cleveland Plain Dealer*.

1916.

Frederick B. Artz, who has been teaching at Antioch College, has been accepted as a member of the Youngstown Hospital Base Unit, which leaves for service in France very soon.

1916 O. T. S.

Born, to Mr. and Mrs. Frank Cary, April 8, 1917, at Tokyo, Japan, a daughter, Helen Emerson.

FORMER STUDENTS.

George W. Norrick is a student at Western Reserve University.

Necrology

˙ELIAS T. JONES, 1859.

Elias T. Jones died at his late residence, 155 South Main Street, Oberlin, May 12, 1917. Mr. Jones was born at Raleigh, North Carolina, June 9, 1834. He came to Oberlin in 1843. He was graduated from the College with the class of 1859. Of this class Professor G. F. Wright is the only surviving male member. Mr. Jones taught in various places, and about twenty-four years ago he returned to Oberlin, where he has made his home. He was married August 12, 1843, to Mrs. Blanche Harris Brooks, who survives him.

MRS. LENORE ROSE FISHBACK, 1905.

Mrs. Lenore Rose Fishback died at Orange, California, April 19, 1917. Mrs. Fishback was born at Kipton, Ohio, June 6, 1883. Her parents moved to Oberlin that she might more advantageously take her college work. She was graduated with the class of 1905 and the following year received the degree of A.M.

She taught from 1906 to 1910 in Atlantic Mine, Michigan, Oberlin, Needles, and Orange, California. She was married at Charter, California, to Mr. M. M. Fishback.

MRS. MABEL WOODSIDE STOKEY, 1907.

Mrs. Mabel Woodside Stokey died at Chicopee, Massachusetts, May 6, 1917. Mrs. Stokey was born at Chicago, Illinois, January 12, 1884. She prepared for Oberlin College in the high school of Oberlin and the Oberlin Academy, and was graduated from College with the class of 1907. In September she began the study of Medicine at the American Medical Missionary College at Battle Creek. In September, 1910, she sailed for Africa, where she served as a medical missionary until a short time ago, when ill health compelled her to return to the United States. She was married May 30, 1913, to Dr. F. E. Stokey at Belmont, Angola, Africa.

THE NATION

20 Vesey Street, New York
$4.00 a year

Never has there been a greater need for a thoughtful, even-tempered periodical, free from sensationalism, bitterness and prejudice. Such a periodical is

The Nation

a weekly journal of Literature, Drama, Art, Music, Science, Finance and Politics. For over fifty years America's Foremost Critical Review.

Kindergarten---Primary Training Course. Oberlin, O.

An accredited school offering a two-year course in the theory and practice of kindergarten and primary teaching.

An attractive professional course of much cultural value.

Advantages of a college town.

For catalogue address the Secretary,

MISS ROSE M. DEAN
Goodrich House, 125 Elm St.

Neōlin Soles Will Last and Comfort You

IT'S summertime — vacation time — beach time—tramping time—

It's time for Neōlin Soles, those advanced, synthetic shoe soles that will inevitably displace leather.

Why are Neōlin Soles summer soles—as well as winter soles? Because their wear-resistance gives them a lasting quality built in and pressed in by titan machines till they're solid, solid wear.

Because Neōlin Soles, though so wear-resisting, are so springy, so buoyant, so flexible that they are foot ideal for knock-about vacationing.

Because Neōlin's peculiar ground-grip tread is good for golf and good for tennis.

Because Neōlin waterproofness is good for the fishing trip and good for the sea-shore. Good for you. Good for the children whose shoe bills it saves, saves, saves.

Neōlin comes in all sizes. In black, white, tan. Search for the stamped name under each Neōlin Sole—and insist upon Neōlin. Be sure to *mark* that mark; stamp it on your memory: neōlın —

the trade symbol for a never changing quality product of

The Goodyear Tire & Rubber Company
Akron, Ohio

neōlin

Trade Mark Reg. U. S. Pat. Off.

Better than Leather

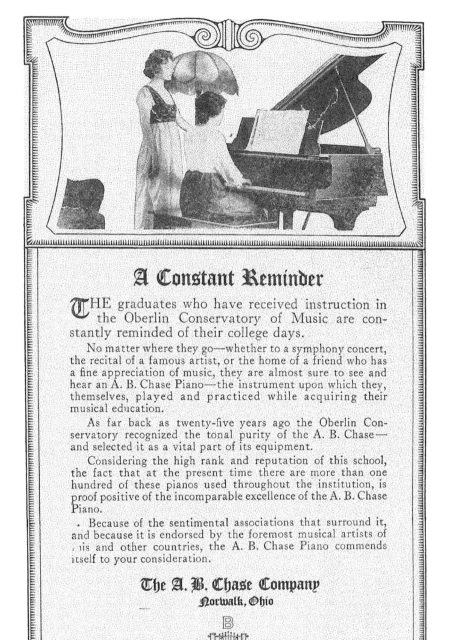

A Constant Reminder

THE graduates who have received instruction in the Oberlin Conservatory of Music are constantly reminded of their college days.

No matter where they go—whether to a symphony concert, the recital of a famous artist, or the home of a friend who has a fine appreciation of music, they are almost sure to see and hear an A. B. Chase Piano—the instrument upon which they, themselves, played and practiced while acquiring their musical education.

As far back as twenty-five years ago the Oberlin Conservatory recognized the tonal purity of the A. B. Chase—and selected it as a vital part of its equipment.

Considering the high rank and reputation of this school, the fact that at the present time there are more than one hundred of these pianos used throughout the institution, is proof positive of the incomparable excellence of the A. B. Chase Piano.

Because of the sentimental associations that surround it, and because it is endorsed by the foremost musical artists of this and other countries, the A. B. Chase Piano commends itself to your consideration.

The A. B. Chase Company
Norwalk, Ohio

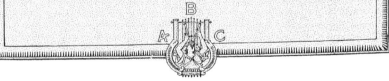

CPSIA information can be obtained
at www.ICGtesting.com
Printed in the USA
BVHW041121211218
536175BV00005B/50/P